INCLUDES THE JOYFUL, LUMINOUS,
SORROWFUL, & GLORIOUS MYSTERIES

A ROSARY
FOR PEACE

UNITED STATES CONFERENCE OF CATHOLIC BISHOPS
WASHINGTON, D.C.

T he document *A Rosary for Peace* was developed as a resource by the Committee on the Liturgy of the United States Conference of Catholic Bishops (USCCB). This revised edition was reviewed by the committee chairman, Cardinal Francis George, OMI, and has been authorized for publication by the undersigned.

Msgr. William P. Fay
General Secretary, USCCB

Excerpts from the English translation of *Rite of Holy Week* © 1972, International Committee on English in the Liturgy, Inc. (ICEL); excerpts from the English translation of *The Roman Missal* © 1973, ICEL; excerpts from the English translation of *The Liturgy of the Hours* © 1974, ICEL; excerpts from the English translation of *A Book of Prayers* © 1982, ICEL; excerpts from the English translation of *Collection of Masses of the Blessed Virgin Mary* © 1989, ICEL. All rights reserved.

First Printing, April 2002
Revised Edition, September 2003

ISBN 1-57455-571-5

Opening Prayers

I n the name of the Father (+), and of the
Son, and of the Holy Spirit. Amen.

*A child is born for us, a son is given to us,
and he shall be called "Prince of Peace."*

SEE ISAIAH 9:6
THE BLESSED VIRGIN MARY, QUEEN OF PEACE,
ENTRANCE ANTIPHON

APOSTLES' CREED

I believe in God, the Father almighty, creator of
    heaven and earth.
I believe in Jesus Christ, his only Son, our Lord.
He was conceived by the power of the Holy Spirit
    and born of the Virgin Mary.
He suffered under Pontius Pilate, was crucified,
    died, and was buried.
He descended into hell.
On the third day he rose again.
He ascended into heaven and is seated at the
    right hand of the Father.
He will come again to judge the living and
    the dead.
I believe in the Holy Spirit, the holy catholic
    Church, the communion of saints, the
    forgiveness of sins, the resurrection of the
    body, and the life everlasting. Amen.

A virgin has given birth to one who is truly God and
*   truly human:*
God has restored our peace, reconciling in himself earth
*   with heaven.*

THE BLESSED VIRGIN MARY, QUEEN OF PEACE,
COMMUNION ANTIPHON

OUR FATHER

Our Father who art in heaven,
hallowed be thy name.
Thy kingdom come.
Thy will be done on earth, as it is in heaven.
Give us this day our daily bread,
and forgive us our trespasses,
as we forgive those who trepass against us,
and lead us not into temptation,
but deliver us from evil.

*Through the intercession
of Blessed Mary, ever Virgin,
grant that our times may be tranquil.*

THE BLESSED VIRGIN MARY, QUEEN OF PEACE, COLLECT

HAIL MARY

Hail Mary, full of grace,
the Lord is with you!
Blessed are you among women,
and blessed is the fruit of your womb, Jesus.
Holy Mary, Mother of God,
pray for us sinners,
now and at the hour of our death.

Through the intercession
of Blessed Mary, ever Virgin,
grant that we may live in peace as one family.

THE BLESSED VIRGIN MARY, QUEEN OF PEACE, COLLECT

Hail Mary . . .

Through the intercession
of Blessed Mary, ever Virgin,
grant that we may be united in love.

THE BLESSED VIRGIN MARY, QUEEN OF PEACE, COLLECT

Hail Mary . . .

Through the intercession
of our Lady, Queen of Peace,
may you strengthen us
to build up in our world
the peace that Christ left us.

THE BLESSED VIRGIN MARY, QUEEN OF PEACE,
PRAYER AFTER COMMUNION

Glory be to the Father, and to the Son, and to the
    Holy Spirit;
as it was in the beginning, is now, and will be
    for ever. Amen.

Joyful Mysteries

Our Father . . .

The Virgin Mary received the angel's message in faith.

ANNUNCIATION OF THE LORD, PREFACE

Hail Mary . . .

In Christ, the hope of all peoples,
our hope was realized beyond all expectation.

BLESSED VIRGIN MARY AND THE
ANNUNCIATION OF THE LORD, PREFACE

Hail Mary . . .

Lord,
strengthen our faith and hope in Jesus, born of a virgin.

ANNUNCIATION OF THE LORD, PRAYER AFTER COMMUNION

Hail Mary . . .

Let the clouds rain down the Just One,
and the earth bring forth the Savior.

SEE ISAIAH 45:8; BLESSED VIRGIN MARY AND THE
ANNUNCIATION OF THE LORD, ENTRANCE ANTIPHON

Hail Mary . . .

The eternal Father sent his angel to bring Mary the
good news of our salvation.

ANNUNCIATION OF THE LORD,
EVENING PRAYER I, INTERCESSIONS

Hail Mary . . .

You sent Gabriel to give Mary your message
    of peace and joy,
give to the world the joy of salvation and
    your gift of true peace.

ANNUNCIATION OF THE LORD,
EVENING PRAYER I, INTERCESSIONS

Hail Mary . . .

Lord our God, you alone work wonders and with you
    all things are possible.

ANNUNCIATION OF THE LORD,
EVENING PRAYER I, INTERCESSIONS

Hail Mary . . .

We celebrate the beginning of our salvation when the
    coming of the Lord was announced by the angel.

ANNUNCIATION OF THE LORD,
MORNING PRAYER, INTERCESSIONS

Hail Mary . . .

May we become more like Jesus Christ,
whom we acknowledge as our redeemer.

ANNUNCIATION OF THE LORD, COLLECT

Hail Mary . . .

You look with love on the humble, and fill the
    hungry with your gifts,
raise up the downcast, help all in need.

ANNUNCIATION OF THE LORD,
EVENING PRAYER II, INTERCESSIONS

Hail Mary . . .

Glory be . . .

Our Father . . .

What wonders you have worked throughout the world.
All generations have shared the greatness of your love.

Blessed Virgin Mary, Preface II

Hail Mary . . .

Eternal Father,
you inspired the Virgin Mary, the mother of your Son.
Keep us open to the working of your Spirit.

Visitation, Collect

Hail Mary . . .

May we always recognize with joy
the presence of Christ.

Visitation, Prayer After Communion

Hail Mary . . .

In obedience
to the inspiration of the Holy Spirit,
may we bring Christ to others.

Visitation of the Blessed Virgin Mary, Collect

Hail Mary . . .

In obedience
to the inspiration of the Holy Spirit,
may we proclaim your greatness
by the praise of our lips
and the holiness of our lives.

Visitation of the Blessed Virgin Mary, Collect

Hail Mary . . .

Happy are you who have believed,
because the Lord's promises will be
      accomplished in you.

VISITATION, OFFICE OF READINGS, RESPONSORY

Hail Mary . . .

The Lord has chosen her,
his loved one from the beginning.

VISITATION, MORNING PRAYER, RESPONSORY

Hail Mary . . .

Blessed are those who hear the word of God,
      and cherish it in their hearts.

VISITATION, MIDMORNING PRAYER, RESPONSORY

Hail Mary . . .

You made Mary the mother of mercy,
      may all who are faced with trials feel her
      motherly love.

VISITATION, EVENING PRAYER, INTERCESSIONS

Hail Mary . . .

Come, all you who fear God, and hear the great things
      the Lord has done for me.

PSALM 65:16
VISITATION, ENTRANCE ANTIPHON

Hail Mary . . .

Glory be . . .

Our Father . . .

May the God of infinite goodness
scatter the darkness of sin
and brighten your hearts with holiness.

CHRISTMAS, MASS AT MIDNIGHT,
PRAYER OVER THE PEOPLE

Hail Mary . . .

Your Son shared our weakness:
may we share his glory.

CHRISTMAS, MASS DURING THE DAY, COLLECT

Hail Mary . . .

Almighty God,
the saving work of Christ
made our peace with you.

CHRISTMAS, MASS DURING THE DAY,
PRAYER OVER THE GIFTS

Hail Mary . . .

In Christ we see our God made visible
and so are caught up in love of the God we cannot see.

CHRISTMAS, PREFACE I

Hail Mary . . .

He has come to lift up all things to himself,
to restore unity to creation.

CHRISTMAS, PREFACE II

Hail Mary . . .

He comes in splendor, the King who is our peace;
the whole world longs to see him.

CHRISTMAS, EVENING PRAYER I, ANTIPHON I

Hail Mary . . .

A new day dawns,
the day of our redemption, prepared by
God from ages past,
the beginning of our never ending gladness.

CHRISTMAS, OFFICE OF READINGS, RESPONSORY

Hail Mary . . .

You are the eternal Word of God who flooded
the world with joy at your birth,
fill us with joy by the continuous gift of your life.

CHRISTMAS, MORNING PRAYER, INTERCESSIONS

Hail Mary . . .

At the birth of Jesus, angels proclaimed
peace to the world.

CHRISTMAS, EVENING PRAYER II, INTERCESSIONS

Hail Mary . . .

Make us faithful to your Word,
that we may bring your life to the waiting world.

CHRISTMAS, EVENING PRAYER II,
ALTERNATIVE PRAYER

Hail Mary . . .

Glory be . . .

THE FOURTH DECADE
MEDITATE ON THE MYSTERY OF THE
PRESENTATION OF THE LORD

Our Father . . .

With my own eyes I have seen the salvation
which you have prepared in the sight of every people.

PRESENTATION OF THE LORD, BLESSING OF
CANDLES AND PROCESSION, ANTIPHON

Hail Mary . . .

Your praise reaches to the ends of the earth;
your right hand is filled with justice.

PSALM 47:11
PRESENTATION OF THE LORD, ENTRANCE ANTIPHON

Hail Mary . . .

Our hearts are joyful,
for we have seen your salvation.

PRESENTATION OF THE LORD, PREFACE

Hail Mary . . .

We too should carry a light for all to see and
reflect the radiance of the true light as we
hasten to meet him.

PRESENTATION OF THE LORD, OFFICE OF READINGS,
FROM A SERMON BY ST. SOPHRONIUS

Hail Mary . . .

Simeon, the just man, took Christ into his arms when
*   he came to the temple,*
help us to welcome Christ in our brothers and sisters.

PRESENTATION OF THE LORD,
MORNING PRAYER, INTERCESSIONS

Hail Mary . . .

The Lord has remembered his gracious promise.
And has kept faith with his people Israel.

PRESENTATION OF THE LORD,
MIDMORNING PRAYER, RESPONSORY

Hail Mary . . .

You are the light that enlightens all nations.

PRESENTATION OF THE LORD,
EVENING PRAYER II, INTERCESSIONS

Hail Mary . . .

May your Church proclaim your salvation to the ends
of the earth.

PRESENTATION OF THE LORD,
EVENING PRAYER II, INTERCESSIONS

Hail Mary . . .

This child is destined for the fall and for the
rising of many.

PRESENTATION OF THE LORD,
OFFICE OF READINGS, ANTIPHON I

Hail Mary . . .

We have now become the people of God.
Our eyes have seen God incarnate.

PRESENTATION OF THE LORD, OFFICE OF READINGS,
FROM A SERMON BY ST. SOPHRONIUS

Hail Mary . . .

Glory be . . .

Our Father . . .

After three days, Jesus was found in the temple, seated in the midst of the doctors, listening to them and asking them questions.

HOLY FAMILY, EVENING PRAYER II, ANTIPHON I

Hail Mary . . .

Eternal Father,
we want to live as Jesus, Mary, and Joseph,
in peace with you and one another.

HOLY FAMILY, PRAYER AFTER COMMUNION

Hail Mary . . .

Establish our families in mutual love and peace.

HOLY FAMILY, EVENING PRAYER I, INTERCESSIONS

Hail Mary . . .

Come, let us worship Christ, the Son of God, who was obedient to Mary and Joseph.

HOLY FAMILY, OFFICE OF READINGS,
INVITATORY, ANTIPHON

Hail Mary . . .

Christ was eager to be about his Father's business.

HOLY FAMILY, EVENING PRAYER I,
INTERCESSIONS

Hail Mary . . .

His father and mother were full of wonder at what was said about their child.

HOLY FAMILY, MORNING PRAYER,
ANTIPHON III

Hail Mary . . .

They looked for Christ among their relatives and friends.

HOLY FAMILY, EVENING PRAYER I,
ANTIPHON FOR THE CANTICLE OF MARY

Hail Mary . . .

Have a rejoicing heart, try to grow holy, help one another, keep united, live in peace.

HOLY FAMILY, OFFICE OF READINGS, RESPONSORY

Hail Mary . . .

Did you not know that I had to be in my Father's house?

HOLY FAMILY, EVENING PRAYER II,
ANTIPHON FOR THE CANTICLE OF MARY

Hail Mary . . .

Bring us to the joy and peace of your eternal home.

HOLY FAMILY, COLLECT

Hail Mary . . .

Glory be . . .

Luminous Mysteries

Our Father . . .

*As soon as Jesus was baptized he came out of the water
and the heavens opened before him.*

BAPTISM OF THE LORD, ANTIPHON, EVENING PRAYER I

Hail Mary . . .

*Father in heaven,
you revealed Christ as your Son
by the voice that spoke over the waters of the Jordan.*

BAPTISM OF THE LORD, ALTERNATIVE OPENING PRAYER

Hail Mary . . .

*I have seen and have given witness that this is the Son
of God.*

BAPTISM OF THE LORD, COMMUNION ANTIPHON

Hail Mary . . .

*Your voice was heard from heaven
to awaken faith in the presence among us
of the Word made man.*

BAPTISM OF THE LORD, PREFACE

Hail Mary . . .

*Your Spirit was seen as a dove,
revealing Jesus as your servant,
and anointing him with joy as the Christ,*

sent to bring to the poor
the good news of salvation.

BAPTISM OF THE LORD, PREFACE

Hail Mary . . .

Through the Blessed Virgin Mary
you revealed your Son to the world
as the glory of Israel
and the light of all nations.

MARY AND THE EPIPHANY OF THE LORD, OPENING PRAYER

Hail Mary . . .

Upon him my spirit will rest.
And he will show all nations the holiness of God.

BAPTISM OF THE LORD, MIDAFTERNOON PRAYER, RESPONSORY

Hail Mary . . .

Christ, you made your light shine on us by revealing
yourself, grant us the spirit of humble service to
all people.

BAPTISM OF THE LORD, MORNING PRAYER, INTERCESSIONS

Hail Mary . . .

Keep us, your children born of water and the Spirit,
faithful to our calling.

BAPTISM OF THE LORD, OPENING PRAYER

Hail Mary . . .

Christ is baptized, the world is made holy.

BAPTISM OF THE LORD, MORNING PRAYER,
ANTIPHON FOR THE CANTICLE OF ZECHARIAH

Hail Mary . . .

Glory be . . .

Our Father . . .

At Cana in Galilee Jesus worked the first of the signs which revealed his glory.

SATURDAY BETWEEN EPIPHANY AND THE BAPTISM OF THE LORD, MORNING PRAYER, ANTIPHON FOR THE CANTICLE OF ZECHARIAH

Hail Mary . . .

In this great sign
the presence of the Messiah is proclaimed.

OUR LADY OF CANA, PREFACE

Hail Mary . . .

In this great sign
the outpouring of the Spirit is foretold.

OUR LADY OF CANA, PREFACE

Hail Mary . . .

In this great sign
the hour of salvation is foreshadowed.

OUR LADY OF CANA, PREFACE

Hail Mary . . .

Blessed are you, Virgin Mary: through you your Son gave the first of his signs.

OUR LADY OF CANA, COMMUNION ANTIPHON

Hail Mary . . .

This mystery, which has been hidden through all ages
and from all generations, is now revealed to us.

SATURDAY BETWEEN EPIPHANY AND THE BAPTISM OF THE LORD,
MIDMORNING PRAYER, ANTIPHON

Hail Mary . . .

Christ Jesus has come, bringing the joyful news of
peace to those who were far off;
peace to those who are near.

SATURDAY BETWEEN EPIPHANY AND THE BAPTISM OF THE LORD,
MIDDAY PRAYER, ANTIPHON

Hail Mary . . .

All nations will see the glory of your holy One.

SATURDAY BETWEEN EPIPHANY AND THE BAPTISM OF THE LORD,
MIDDAY PRAYER, RESPONSORY

Hail Mary . . .

She is the Virgin of prayer,
who shows concern for the bridegroom and bride of
Cana and intercedes for them with her Son.

MARY, IMAGE AND MOTHER OF THE CHURCH II, PREFACE

Hail Mary . . .

Grant that by heeding the words of Christ's mother
we may do what he commands us
in the Gospel he has given us.

OUR LADY OF CANA, OPENING PRAYER

Hail Mary . . .

Glory be . . .

Our Father . . .

*Jesus preached the Gospel of the kingdom and cured
those who were in need of healing.*

THIRD SUNDAY IN ORDINARY TIME, EVENING PRAYER I,
ANTIPHON FOR THE CANTICLE OF MARY

Hail Mary . . .

*As the first disciple of her Son
[Mary] receives the message of the Gospel.*

OUR LADY OF NAZARETH, PREFACE

Hail Mary . . .

*Hail, full of grace; you are called upon by sinners
because you are merciful.*

MARY, MOTHER OF RECONCILIATION, ENTRANCE ANTIPHON

Hail Mary . . .

*Relying on the help of the Blessed Virgin Mary
we ask that we may cast aside the old ways of sin
and put on Jesus Christ.*

MARY, HELP OF CHRISTIANS, PRAYER AFTER COMMUNION

Hail Mary . . .

*Seeing [Mary's] beauty of spirit,
[may we] turn away from sin in its ugliness;
taking to heart her words and example,
[may we] learn to keep your Son's commandments.*

MARY, MOTHER OF RECONCILIATION, PREFACE

Hail Mary . . .

Strengthen your faithful people,
so that we may seek your kingdom and its justice.

MARY, MOTHER OF DIVINE PROVIDENCE, PRAYER AFTER COMMUNION

Hail Mary . . .

Grant that, through [Mary's] prayers and help,
we may always live as good citizens of this world,
with our hearts fixed on the world to come.

MARY, MOTHER OF DIVINE HOPE, OPENING PRAYER

Hail Mary . . .

Hail, holy Mother! The child to whom you gave birth
    is the king of heaven and earth forever.

COMMON OF THE BLESSED VIRGIN MARY I, ENTRANCE ANTIPHON

Hail Mary . . .

Through the example
of the Blessed Virgin Mary,
[grant that] we may work silently
at building up your kingdom on earth
and so enjoy its fulfillment in heaven.

OUR LADY OF NAZARETH, PRAYER AFTER COMMUNION

Hail Mary . . .

As king he claims dominion over all creation,
that he may present to you, his almighty Father,
an eternal and universal kingdom:
a kingdom of truth and life,
a kingdom of holiness and grace,
a kingdom of justice, love, and peace.

CHRIST THE KING, PREFACE

Hail Mary . . .

Glory be . . .

How to Pray the Rosary

Opening Prayers:

1. Make the Sign of the Cross with the crucifix of the rosary.
2. Say the "*Apostles' Creed*".
3. On the 1st bead from the crucifix, say one "*Our Father*".
4. On the 2nd, 3rd and 4th beads, say the "*Hail Mary*".
5. Say one "*Glory Be to the Father*".

For each of the 5 decades:

6. Announce the Mystery.
7. On the large bead before each decade, say one "*Our Father*".
8. Say ten "*Hail Marys*", (one for each small bead of the decade) while meditating on the Mystery.
9. Say the "*Glory Be to the Father*".

After each decade:

10. Say the following prayer requested by the Blessed Virgin Mary at Fatima:
"O my Jesus, forgive us our sins, save us from the fires of hell. Lead all souls to Heaven, especially those in most need of Your mercy".

Closing prayer:

11. Say the "*Hail, Holy Queen*".

MR-04

Mysteries of the Holy Rosary

JOYFUL MYSTERIES
(Monday, Saturday)

Annunciation

Visitation

Birth of Jesus

Presentation in the Temple

Finding the Child Jesus

SORROWFUL MYSTERIES
(Tuesday, Friday)

Agony in the Garden

Scourging at the Pillar

Crowning with Thorns

Carrying of the Cross

Crucifixion

GLORIOUS MYSTERIES
(Wednesday, Sunday)

Resurrection

Ascension into Heaven

Descent of the Holy Spirit

Assumption

Crowning of Our Blessed Lady

MYSTERIES OF LIGHT
(Thursday)

Christ's Baptism in the Jordan

Wedding at Cana

Proclamation of the Kingdom

Transfiguration

Institution of the Eucharist

Our Father . . .

*Jesus took his disciples and went up the mountain
where he was transfigured before them.*

TRANSFIGURATION, EVENING PRAYER I, ANTIPHON

Hail Mary . . .

*A voice spoke from the cloud: This is my beloved Son in
whom I am well pleased; listen to him.*

TRANSFIGURATION, MORNING PRAYER,
ANTIPHON FOR THE CANTICLE OF ZECHARIAH

Hail Mary . . .

*He revealed his glory to the disciples
to strengthen them for the scandal of the cross.*

TRANSFIGURATION, PREFACE

Hail Mary . . .

*Lord,
you revealed the true radiance of Christ
in the glory of his transfiguration.*

TRANSFIGURATION, PRAYER AFTER COMMUNION

Hail Mary . . .

*Strengthen our faith
by confirming the witness of your prophets,
and show us the splendor of your beloved sons
and daughters.*

TRANSFIGURATION, OPENING PRAYER

Hail Mary . . .

Christ Jesus, . . . you sustain all creation with your
powerful word and cleanse us of all our sins.

TRANSFIGURATION, EVENING PRAYER I,
ANTIPHON FOR THE CANTICLE OF MARY

Hail Mary . . .

O God, you have scattered the darkness with your light
and have poured your light into our hearts.

TRANSFIGURATION, MORNING PRAYER, INTERCESSIONS

Hail Mary . . .

Give joy and peace to all peoples
and fill our hearts with the light of your holiness.

MARY, MOTHER OF FAIREST LOVE, OPENING PRAYER

Hail Mary . . .

May Mary's prayers help to free us from all evils here
on earth
and lead us to eternal joy in heaven.

PRAYERS FOR MASSES OF THE
BLESSED VIRGIN MARY, OPENING PRAYER

Hail Mary . . .

Grant that like [Mary]
we may seek only what is true and just
and so come before you, the origin of all beauty
and the author of purest love.

MARY, MOTHER OF FAIREST LOVE, OPENING PRAYER

Hail Mary . . .

Glory be . . .

Our Father . . .

While they were at supper, Jesus took bread, said the
blessing, broke the bread and gave it to his disciples.

HOLY THURSDAY, EVENING PRAYER,
ANTIPHON FOR THE CANTICLE OF MARY

Hail Mary . . .

Christ invites all to the supper in which he gives his
body and blood for the life of the world.

BODY AND BLOOD OF CHRIST,
EVENING PRAYER I, INTERCESSIONS

Hail Mary . . .

Christ, bread from heaven, you form one body out of all
who partake of the one bread, refresh all who
believe in you with harmony and peace.

BODY AND BLOOD OF CHRIST,
EVENING PRAYER I, INTERCESSIONS

Hail Mary . . .

The love of Christ has gathered us together into one.

MASS OF THE LORD'S SUPPER, ANTIPHON,
PROCESSION, LITURGY OF THE EUCHARIST

Hail Mary . . .

Let us take heed not to be divided in mind.
Let there be an end to bitterness and quarrels, an end
to strife,
and in our midst be Christ our God.

MASS OF THE LORD'S SUPPER, ANTIPHON,
PROCESSION, LITURGY OF THE EUCHARIST

Hail Mary . . .

May we offer to our Father in heaven
a solemn pledge of undivided love.

BODY AND BLOOD OF CHRIST,
ALTERNATIVE OPENING PRAYER

Hail Mary . . .

May we offer to our brothers and sisters
a life poured out in loving service of [the] kingdom.

BODY AND BLOOD OF CHRIST,
ALTERNATIVE OPENING PRAYER

Hail Mary . . .

The Lord brings peace to his Church, and fills us with
the finest wheat.

BODY AND BLOOD OF CHRIST,
EVENING PRAYER I, ANTIPHON

Hail Mary . . .

Grant that under the protection of the Blessed Virgin
we may work for the unity of peace of all those
for who your Son offered himself
as the sacrifice of our redemption

OUR LADY OF THE CENACLE, PRAYER AFTER COMMUNION

Hail Mary . . .

May our worship of this sacrament of your
body and blood
help us to experience the salvation you won for us
and the peace of your kingdom.

BODY AND BLOOD OF CHRIST, OPENING PRAYER

Hail Mary . . .

Glory be . ...

Sorrowful Mysteries

THE FIRST DECADE
MEDITATE ON THE MYSTERY OF THE
AGONY IN THE GARDEN

Our Father . . .

My heart is nearly broken with sorrow; stay here and keep watch with me.

MONDAY OF HOLY WEEK,
MORNING PRAYER, ANTIPHON I

Hail Mary . . .

*Help us to bear witness
by following Christ's example of suffering.*

PASSION SUNDAY, EVENING PRAYER I, PRAYER

Hail Mary . . .

Here I am, Lord God, I come to do your will.

PSALM 40:7-8
PASSION SUNDAY, OFFICE OF READINGS, RESPONSORY

Hail Mary . . .

*You have redeemed us with your precious blood;
hear the prayer of your servants
and come to our help.*

MONDAY OF HOLY WEEK,
OFFICE OF READINGS, RESPONSORY

Hail Mary . . .

25

My soul is in anguish, my heart is in torment.

GOOD FRIDAY, EVENING PRAYER, ANTIPHON II

Hail Mary . . .

*Father, if this cup may not pass, but I must drink it,
     then your will be done.*

MATTHEW 26:42
PASSION SUNDAY, COMMUNION RITE

Hail Mary . . .

*Through her heart, his sorrow sharing,
All his bitter anguish bearing.*

OUR LADY OF SORROWS, SEQUENCE

Hail Mary . . .

*Be glad to share in the sufferings of Christ!
When he comes in glory, you will be filled with joy.*

1 PETER 4:13
OUR LADY OF SORROWS, COMMUNION ANTIPHON

Hail Mary . . .

*Grant that we may bring love and comfort
to our brothers and sisters in distress.*

THE BLESSED VIRGIN MARY AT THE
FOOT OF THE CROSS I, COLLECT

Hail Mary . . .

*For the sake of you, who left a garden, I was betrayed
in a garden.*

HOLY SATURDAY, OFFICE OF READINGS,
FROM AN ANCIENT HOMILY ON HOLY SATURDAY

Hail Mary . . .

Glory be . . .

THE SECOND DECADE
MEDITATE ON THE MYSTERY OF THE
SCOURGING AT THE PILLAR

Our Father . . .

Now you come to scourge me and lead me to the cross.

PASSION SUNDAY, EVENING PRAYER I, ANTIPHON I

Hail Mary . . .

Christ was scourged and treated with contempt,
but God's right hand has raised him up.

PASSION SUNDAY, EVENING PRAYER II, ANTIPHON I

Hail Mary . . .

On my back see the marks of the scourging
I endured to remove the burden of sin that
weighs upon your back.

HOLY SATURDAY, OFFICE OF READINGS,
FROM AN ANCIENT HOMILY ON HOLY SATURDAY

Hail Mary . . .

Bruised, derided, cursed, defiled,
She beheld her tender Child,
All with bloody scourges rent.

OUR LADY OF SORROWS, SEQUENCE

Hail Mary . . .

Though he was sinless, he suffered willingly for sinners.

PASSION SUNDAY, PREFACE

Hail Mary . . .

He offered himself as a victim for our deliverance.

HOLY EUCHARIST, PREFACE I

Hail Mary . . .

By your own blood, Lord, you brought us back to God.

PASSION SUNDAY, MORNING PRAYER, RESPONSORY

Hail Mary . . .

*The Father of mercies has given us an example of
    unselfish love
in the sufferings of his only Son.*

PASSION SUNDAY, PRAYER OVER THE PEOPLE

Hail Mary . . .

*He humbled himself for our sakes;
may you follow his example.*

PASSION SUNDAY, PRAYER OVER THE PEOPLE

Hail Mary . . .

*I fill out in my flesh what is lacking in the
suffering of Christ, for the sake of his Body,
which is the Church.*

THE BLESSED VIRGIN MARY AT THE
FOOT OF THE CROSS I, COMMUNION ANTIPHON

Hail Mary . . .

Glory be . . .

Our Father . . .

The head that once was crown'd with thorns
Is crown'd with glory now.

EXALTATION OF THE HOLY CROSS,
OFFICE OF READINGS, HYMN

Hail Mary . . .

Christ is the King of all creation.

CHRIST THE KING, PRAYER AFTER COMMUNION

Hail Mary . . .

Have mercy on us for whose sake you endured so much.

MONDAY OF HOLY WEEK,
OFFICE OF READINGS, RESPONSORY

Hail Mary . . .

You will rule over all.

CHRIST THE KING, EVENING PRAYER I, RESPONSORY

Hail Mary . . .

You choose the weak and make them strong
in bearing witness to you.

PREFACE OF MARTYRS

Hail Mary . . .

You have entered on the way that the Lord has graciously opened up for you, until you receive the crown of glory.

COMMON OF SEVERAL MARTYRS, OFFICE OF READINGS,
FROM A LETTER BY SAINT CYPRIAN, BISHOP AND MARTYR

Hail Mary . . .

*I have kept the faith;
now a crown of holiness awaits me.*

COMMON OF ONE MARTYR,
OFFICE OF READINGS, RESPONSORY

Hail Mary . . .

By your own blood, Lord, you brought us back to God.

MONDAY OF HOLY WEEK,
MORNING PRAYER, RESPONSORY

Hail Mary . . .

The Lord will bless his people with peace.

CHRIST THE KING,
MIDMORNING PRAYER, RESPONSORY

Hail Mary . . .

Come let us worship Jesus Christ, the King of Kings.

CHRIST THE KING, INVITATORY

Hail Mary . . .

Glory be . . .

Our Father . . .

Jesus Christ accepted the cross
and freed us from the power of the enemy.

WEDNESDAY OF HOLY WEEK, COLLECT

Hail Mary . . .

If anyone wishes to come after me, he must deny
himself, take up his cross, and follow me.

COMMON OF ONE MARTYR,
EVENING PRAYER II, ANTIPHON I

Hail Mary . . .

Through the cross you brought joy to the world.

GOOD FRIDAY, SONG AT THE
VENERATION OF THE CROSS

Hail Mary . . .

Lord,
by the suffering of Christ your Son
you have saved us all from death.

GOOD FRIDAY, PRAYER

Hail Mary . . .

See the cross of the Lord; let all his enemies flee.

EXALTATION OF THE HOLY CROSS,
OFFICE OF READINGS, ANTIPHON I

Hail Mary . . .

If we share fully in the sufferings of Christ,
through Christ we shall know the fullness of
his consolation.

Hail Mary . . .

You suffered for us; have mercy on us.

Hail Mary . . .

Grant that by carrying our cross each day
we may come to share in his resurrection.

Hail Mary . . .

Though innocent, he accepted death to save the guilty.

Hail Mary . . .

Lord, through your cross bring us to the glory of
*   your kingdom.*

Hail Mary . . .

Glory be . . .

Our Father . . .

We must glory in the cross of our Lord Jesus Christ.

EXALTATION OF THE HOLY CROSS,
EVENING PRAYER I, ANTIPHON III

Hail Mary . . .

*Christ our Savior, on the cross you embraced all time
with your outstretched arms.*

GOOD FRIDAY, MORNING PRAYER, INTERCESSIONS

Hail Mary . . .

*O Christ, you humbled yourself and became obedient
unto death, even death on a cross.*

EXALTATION OF THE HOLY CROSS,
EVENING PRAYER I, INTERCESSIONS

Hail Mary . . .

*The death of your Son gives us hope and strengthens
our faith.*

PASSION SUNDAY,
PRAYER AFTER COMMUNION

Hail Mary . . .

*We worship you, O Christ, and we praise you;
because by your cross you have redeemed the world.*

GOOD FRIDAY,
MIDMORNING PRAYER, RESPONSORY

Hail Mary . . .

Father, into your hands, I commend my spirit.

HANDBOOK OF INDULGENCES,
PIOUS INVOCATION

Hail Mary . . .

*Through his cross, Christ our peace has reconciled
us to God.*

OUR LADY OF SORROWS,
EVENING PRAYER, ANTIPHON I

Hail Mary . . .

*At the cross with motherly love
she embraces her scattered children,
reunited through the death of Christ.*

THE BLESSED VIRGIN MARY AT THE
FOOT OF THE CROSS I, PREFACE

Hail Mary . . .

Raise us up to share in the triumph of your cross.

EXALTATION OF THE HOLY CROSS,
MORNING PRAYER, INTERCESSIONS

Hail Mary . . .

*Christ our life, by your death on the cross you destroyed
the power of evil and death.*

GOOD FRIDAY, MORNING PRAYER, INTERCESSIONS

Hail Mary . . .

Glory be . . .

Glorious Mysteries

Our Father . . .

*All times belong to him
and all the ages.*

INSCRIPTION OF THE PASCHAL CANDLE

Hail Mary . . .

*By his holy and glorious wounds
may Christ our Lord
guard us and keep us.*

INSCRIPTION OF THE PASCHAL CANDLE

Hail Mary . . .

*May the light of Christ, rising in glory,
dispel the darkness of our hearts and minds.*

INSCRIPTION OF THE PASCHAL CANDLE

Hail Mary . . .

*Christ has conquered! Glory fills you!
Darkness vanishes for ever!*

EXSULTET

Hail Mary . . .

*Christ has ransomed us with his blood
and paid for us the price of Adam's sin
to our eternal Father!*

EXSULTET

Hail Mary . . .

This is the night when the pillar of fire
destroyed the darkness of sin.

EXSULTET

Hail Mary . . .

The power of this holy night
dispels all evil, washes guilt away,
restores lost innocence, brings mourners joy;
it casts out hatred, brings us peace, and humbles
*   earthly pride.*

EXSULTET

Hail Mary . . .

Christ is the Morning Star, who came back from the dead,
and shed his peaceful light on all mankind.

EXSULTET

Hail Mary . . .

Bring lasting salvation to mankind,
so that the world may see
the fallen lifted up.

EASTER VIGIL, PRAYER AFTER READING VII

Hail Mary . . .

May the old be made new,
and all things brought to perfection.

EASTER VIGIL, PRAYER AFTER READING VII

Hail Mary . . .

Glory be . . .

Our Father . . .

I, the Lord, am with you always, until the end of
the world.

MATTHEW 28:20
ASCENSION OF THE LORD, COMMUNION ANTIPHON

Hail Mary . . .

In the Eucharist
we touch the divine life you gave to the world.

ASCENSION OF THE LORD,
PRAYER AFTER COMMUNION

Hail Mary . . .

Where he has gone, we hope to follow.

ASCENSION OF THE LORD, PREFACE I

Hail Mary . . .

He was taken up to heaven in their sight
to claim for us a share in his divine life.

ASCENSION OF THE LORD, PREFACE II

Hail Mary . . .

You came down from heaven on a pilgrimage of love,
grant that we may take the same path to your presence.

ASCENSION OF THE LORD,
EVENING PRAYER I, INTERCESSIONS

Hail Mary . . .

*The Lord God ascended on high; he has led
captivity captive.*

ASCENSION OF THE LORD,
OFFICE OF READINGS, ANTIPHON II

Hail Mary . . .

*Eternal Priest and minister of the new Covenant,
you live for ever to make intercession for us.*

ASCENSION OF THE LORD,
MORNING PRAYER, INTERCESSIONS

Hail Mary . . .

*May we follow him into the new creation,
for his ascension is our glory and our hope.*

ASCENSION OF THE LORD, COLLECT

Hail Mary . . .

Do not let your hearts be troubled.

ASCENSION OF THE LORD, MIDMORNING PRAYER

Hail Mary . . .

*Do not leave us orphans, but send us the Father's
promised gift, the Spirit of truth.*

ASCENSION OF THE LORD, EVENING PRAYER II,
ANTIPHON FOR THE CANTICLE OF MARY

Hail Mary . . .

Glory be . . .

Our Father . . .

*You sent the Holy Spirit
upon those marked out to be your children.*

PENTECOST, PREFACE

Hail Mary . . .

*You created from the many languages of man
one voice to profess one faith.*

PENTECOST, PREFACE

Hail Mary . . .

*May the Spirit unite the races and nations on the earth
to proclaim your glory.*

VIGIL OF PENTECOST, COLLECT

Hail Mary . . .

*Strengthen us with your Holy Spirit
and fill us with your light.*

VIGIL OF PENTECOST, COLLECT

Hail Mary . . .

*Send your Spirit
to help the Church you love
show your salvation to the world.*

VIGIL OF PENTECOST, PRAYER OVER THE GIFTS

Hail Mary . . .

Send the Holy Spirit of Pentecost into our hearts
to keep us always in your love.

VIGIL OF PENTECOST,
PRAYER AFTER COMMUNION

Hail Mary . . .

Let the Spirit you sent on your Church
work in the world
through the hearts of all who believe.

PENTECOST, COLLECT

Hail Mary . . .

The Spirit of the Lord fills the whole world. It holds all
things together and knows every word spoken by man.

WISDOM 1:7
PENTECOST, ENTRANCE ANTIPHON

Hail Mary . . .

Keep within us the vigor of your Spirit
and protect the gifts you have given your Church.

PENTECOST, PRAYER AFTER COMMUNION

Hail Mary . . .

May that fire that hovered over the disciples
as tongues of flame
burn out all evil from our hearts
and make them glow with pure light.

PENTECOST, PRAYER OVER THE PEOPLE

Hail Mary . . .

Glory be . . .

Our Father . . .

*Today the virgin Mother of God was taken up into
heaven to be a sign of hope and comfort for your people
on their pilgrim way.*

ASSUMPTION OF THE BLESSED VIRGIN MARY, PREFACE

Hail Mary . . .

*All honor to you, Mary! Today you were raised above
the choirs of angels to lasting glory with Christ.*

VIGIL OF THE ASSUMPTION OF THE
BLESSED VIRGIN MARY, ENTRANCE ANTIPHON

Hail Mary . . .

*At the Virgin Mary's assumption the angels rejoice,
giving praise to the Son of God.*

ASSUMPTION OF THE BLESSED VIRGIN MARY,
ENTRANCE ANTIPHON

Hail Mary . . .

*May we see heaven as our final goal
and come to share her glory.*

ASSUMPTION OF THE BLESSED VIRGIN MARY, COLLECT

Hail Mary . . .

*By her prayers, help us to seek you, Lord,
and to live in your love.*

ASSUMPTION OF THE BLESSED VIRGIN MARY,
PRAYER OVER THE GIFTS

Hail Mary . . .

Through Eve the gates of heaven were closed to all mankind; through the Virgin Mother they were opened wide again.

ASSUMPTION OF THE BLESSED VIRGIN MARY,
EVENING PRAYER I, ANTIPHON II

Hail Mary . . .

Through her intercession grant strength to the weak, comfort to the sorrowing, pardon to sinners.

ASSUMPTION OF THE BLESSED VIRGIN MARY,
EVENING PRAYER I, INTERCESSIONS

Hail Mary . . .

Happy are you, holy Virgin Mary, and most worthy of all praise; from your womb Christ the Sun of Justice has risen.

ASSUMPTION OF THE BLESSED VIRGIN MARY,
OFFICE OF READINGS, RESPONSORY

Hail Mary . . .

This daughter of Jerusalem is lovely and beautiful as she ascends to heaven like the rising sun at daybreak.

ASSUMPTION OF THE BLESSED VIRGIN MARY,
MORNING PRAYER ANTIPHON FOR THE GOSPEL CANTICLE

Hail Mary . . .

We share the fruit of life through you, O daughter blessed by the Lord.

ASSUMPTION OF THE BLESSED VIRGIN MARY,
EVENING PRAYER II, ANTIPHON III

Hail Mary . . .

Glory be . . .

THE FIFTH DECADE
MEDITATE ON THE MYSTERY OF THE
CORONATION OF THE BLESSED VIRGIN MARY

Our Father . . .

We fly to your patronage,
O holy Mother of God.

LITURGY OF THE HOURS,
NIGHT PRAYER, SUB TUUM PRAESIDIUM

Hail Mary . . .

To you do we cry,
poor banished children of Eve.

LITURGY OF THE HOURS, NIGHT PRAYER, SALVE REGINA

Hail Mary . . .

To you do we send up our sighs,
mourning and weeping in this valley of tears.

LITURGY OF THE HOURS, NIGHT PRAYER, SALVE REGINA

Hail Mary . . .

Mary,
Mother of grace and Mother of mercy,
shield me from the enemy
and receive me at the hour of my death.

ENCHIRIDION INDULGENTIARUM,
MARIA, MATER GRATIAE

Hail Mary . . .

O Mother of the Word Incarnate,
despise not my petitions,
but in your mercy hear and answer me.

LITURGY OF THE HOURS, NIGHT PRAYER, MEMORARE

Hail Mary . . .

Turn then, most gracious Advocate,
your eyes of mercy toward us.

LITURGY OF THE HOURS, NIGHT PRAYER, SALVE REGINA

Hail Mary . . .

O clement, O loving,
O sweet, Virgin Mary.

LITURGY OF THE HOURS, NIGHT PRAYER, SALVE REGINA

Hail Mary . . .

Holy Mary,
help the helpless,
strengthen the fearful,
comfort the sorrowful.

LITURGY OF THE HOURS, NIGHT PRAYER,
SANCTA MARIA, SUCCURRE MISERIS

Hail Mary . . .

May all who keep your sacred commemoration
experience the might of your assistance.

LITURGY OF THE HOURS, NIGHT PRAYER,
SANCTA MARIA, SUCCURRE MISERIS

Hail Mary . . .

Deliver us always from all dangers,
O glorious and blessed Virgin.

LITURGY OF THE HOURS,
NIGHT PRAYER, SUB TUUM PRAESIDIUM

Hail Mary . . .

Glory be . . .

Closing Prayers

Lord our God,
you chose the mother of your beloved Son
to be the mother and help of Christians;
grant that we may live under her protection
and that your Church may enjoy unbroken peace.

We make our prayer through our Lord Jesus
    Christ, your Son,
who lives and reigns with you and the
    Holy Spirit,
one God, for ever and ever.
Amen.

BLESSED VIRGIN MARY, HELP OF CHRISTIANS, COLLECT

HAIL, HOLY QUEEN

Hail, holy Queen, mother of mercy,
our life, our sweetness, and our hope.
To you do we cry,
poor banished children of Eve.
To you do we send up our sighs
mourning and weeping in this vale of tears.
Turn then, most gracious advocate,
your eyes of mercy toward us,
and after this our exile
show us the blessed fruit of your womb, Jesus.

O clement, O loving,
O sweet Virgin Mary.
Pray for us, O Holy Mother of God,
that we may be made worthy
    of the promises of Christ.